FRANCIS FRITH'S
TOWN&CITY
MEMORIES

WORTHING

RONALD KERRIDGE was born in 1938 and is a life-long Sussex resident. He is married with a daughter, son and three grandchildren. He is a keen local historian with six previous publications to his credit. In 1989 he was awarded his masters degree in regional history. As a retired local government officer he now spends his spare time Lecturing in local history and following his other interests in archaeology and geology.

MICHAEL STANDING was born in 1946 and lived in Worthing until four years ago when he moved to a village near Chichester. He is married and has two sons, a daughter and five much-loved grandchildren. In 1989 he was awarded a Masters Degree with Distinction in Regional History, and with his co-author, Ronald Kerridge, has written 'Georgian and Victorian Broadwater', 'Ferring Past', 'Worthing - From Saxon Settlement to Seaside Town', and 'Sussex Revisited'.

FRANCIS FRITH'S
TOWN & CITY
MEMORIES

WORTHING

RONALD KERRIDGE & MICHAEL STANDING

FRANCIS FRITH'S
TOWN & CITY
MEMORIES

First published as Worthing, A Photographic History of your Town
in 2001 by Black Horse Books, an imprint of The Francis Frith Collection
Revised edition published in the United Kingdom in 2005 by
The Francis Frith Collection as Worthing, Town and City Memories
Limited Hardback Edition ISBN 1-84589-066-3
Paperback Edition ISBN 1-85937-995-8

British Library Cataloguing in Publication Data

Worthing
Town and City Memories
Ronald Kerridge & Michael Standing

The Francis Frith Collection®
Frith's Barn, Teffont,
Salisbury, Wiltshire SP3 5QP
Tel: +44 (0) 1722 716 376
Email: info@francisfrith.co.uk
www.francisfrith.co.uk

Aerial photographs reproduced under licence from Simmons Aerofilms Limited
Historical Ordnance Survey maps reproduced under licence from Homecheck.co.uk

Printed and bound in England

Front Cover: **WORTHING, THE BEACH 1925** 78826t
The colour-tinting in this image is for illustrative purposes only,
and is not intended to be historically accurate

FRANCIS FRITH'S
TOWN & CITY
MEMORIES

CONTENTS

Francis Frith, Victorian founder of the world-famous photographic archive, was a devout Quaker and a highly successful Victorian businessman. By 1860 he was already a multi-millionaire, having established and sold a wholesale grocery business in Liverpool. He had also made a series of pioneering photographic journeys to the Nile region. The images he returned with were the talk of London. An eminent modern historian has likened their impact on the population of the time to that on our own generation of the first photographs taken on the surface of the moon.

Frith had a passion for landscape, and was as equally inspired by the countryside of Britain as he was by the desert regions of the Nile. He resolved to set out on a new career and to use his skills with a camera. He established a business in Reigate as a specialist publisher of topographical photographs.

Frith lived in an era of immense and sometimes violent change. For the poor in the early part of Victoria's reign work was a drudge and the hours long, and ordinary people had precious little free time. Most had not travelled far beyond the boundaries of their own town or village. Mass tourism was in its infancy during the 1860s, but during the next decade the railway network and the establishment of Bank Holidays and half-Saturdays gradually made it possible for the working man and his family to enjoy holidays and to see a little more of the world. With characteristic business acumen, Francis Frith foresaw that these new tourists would enjoy having souvenirs to commemorate their days out. He began selling photo-souvenirs of seaside resorts and beauty spots, which the Victorian public pasted into treasured family albums.

Frith's aim was to photograph every town and village in Britain. For the next thirty years he travelled the country by train and by pony and trap, producing fine photographs of seaside resorts and beauty spots that were keenly bought by millions of Victorians.

THE RISE OF FRITH & CO

Each photograph was taken with tourism in mind, the small team of Frith photographers concentrating on busy shopping streets, beaches, seafronts, picturesque lanes and villages. They also photographed buildings: the Victorian and Edwardian eras were times of huge building activity, and town halls, libraries, post offices, schools and technical colleges were springing up all over the country. They were invariably celebrated by a proud Victorian public, and photo souvenirs – visual records – published by F Frith & Co were sold in their hundreds of thousands. In addition, many new commercial buildings such as hotels, inns and pubs were photographed, often because their owners specifically commissioned Frith postcards or prints of them for re-sale or for publicity purposes.

In order to gain some understanding of the scale of Frith's business one only has to look at the catalogue issued by Frith & Co in 1886: it runs to some 670 pages. By 1890 Frith had created the greatest specialist photographic publishing company in the world, with over 2,000 stockists! The picture on the right shows the Frith & Co display board on the wall of the stockist at Ingleton in the Yorkshire Dales (left of window). Beautifully constructed with a mahogany frame and gilt inserts, it displayed a dozen scenes.

POSTCARD BONANZA

The ever-popular holiday postcard we know today took many years to appear, and F Frith & Co was in the vanguard of its development. Postcards became a hugely popular means of communication and sold in their millions. Frith's company took full advantage of this boom and soon became the major publisher of photographic view postcards.

Francis Frith died in 1898 at his villa in Cannes, his great project still growing. His sons Eustace and Cyril continued their father's monumental task, expanding the number of views offered to the public and recording more and more places in Britain, as the coasts and countryside were opened up to mass travel. The archive Frith created continued in business for another seventy years. By 1970 it contained over a third of a million pictures of 7,000 cities, towns and villages. The massive photographic record Frith has left to us stands as a living monument to a special and very remarkable man.

This book shows Worthing as it was photographed by this world-famous archive at various periods in its development over the past 150 years. Every photograph was taken for a specific commercial purpose, which explains why the selection may not show every aspect of the town landscape. However, the photographs, compiled from one of the world's most celebrated archives, provide an important and absorbing record of your town.

VICTORIAN COUNTY MAP

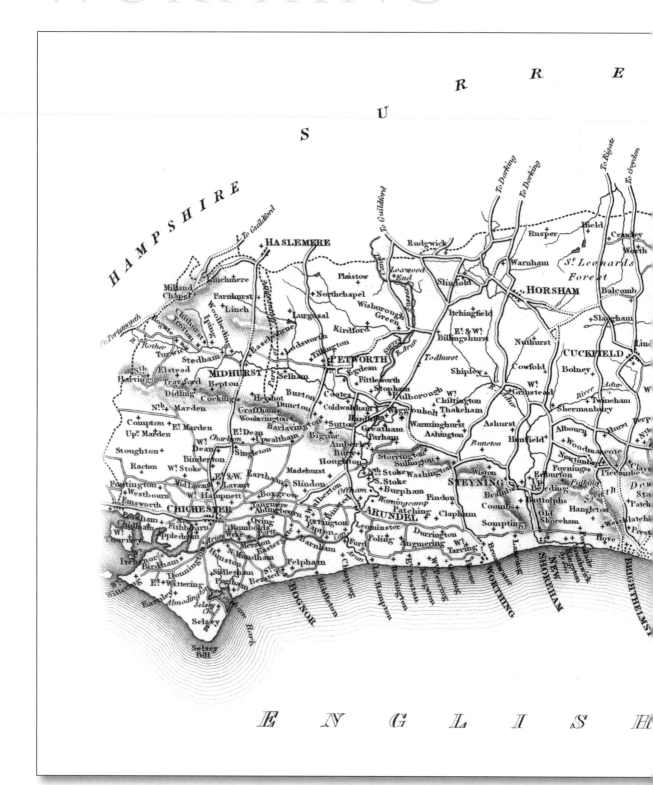

VICTORIAN COUNTY MAP

A VICTORIAN COUNTY MAP OF SUSSEX, SHOWING
WORTHING AND THE SURROUNDING AREAS c1835

During the past two centuries, Worthing has grown from a small isolated fishing and agricultural hamlet, of no more than thirty households, to the large urban conurbation that is today the modern Borough.

Man first settled in the area over 5,000 years ago, when Neolithic man exploited the flints found in the chalk of the South Downs to the north of the modern town; the fertile coastal plain on which the town is located was part of a 'grain factory' for the Roman empire. In the 5th century, Saxon migrants settled near to the numerous tidal creeks, which were very similar to the flooded homelands they had left on the North German and Friesian coast. It is from these migrants that Sussex derives its name: they were quite distinct from those who settled the kingdoms of Kent and Wessex and are described in the Anglo Saxon Chronicles as 'Suose(a)xe', hence Sussex. By the

INTRODUCTION

SOUTH STREET 1899 43956

successful development of seaside resorts. Worthing, with its mild and equable climate, sheltered from the north-east winds by the downs and with a high level of sunshine — especially in winter — was favourably sited. Its gently sloping sandy beach was soon discovered and the town benefited from the limited but growing attraction of sea-bathing. Its popularity received a considerable boost when Princess Amelia, the youngest child of George III, visited in 1798 to cure a lame knee, and a second Royal visit in 1807 by the youthful Princess Charlotte, daughter of the Prince Regent, ensured its status as a fashionable Georgian watering place. Although nearby Brighton was attracting many more visitors, it already had a reputation for noise and disruption, which rendered it unpopular with certain elements of society. This undoubtedly helped to establish Worthing's early reputation as a select resort, and The Times of 28 September 1811 records that the emerging Georgian resort was 'crowded with fashionable visitors during August and September'.

In the years of peace that followed the Napoleonic Wars, the wealthy and fashionable visitors for whom Worthing had exclusively catered during the first quarter of the 19th century abandoned the developing late-Georgian seaside watering places and again went abroad for their recreation. Also, from 1820, other British resorts had started competing with Sussex's emerging coastal resorts, leading to the loss of even more of their established clientele. By 1829, Worthing was nearly bankrupt. Business was at a standstill, hotels were empty and the town's debts and official salaries remained unpaid. The late 18th and early 19th century mode of holiday, with its select company, libraries and assemblies, had completely collapsed.

The visit of Princess Augusta, daughter of George III, during the winter of 1829-30 did little to halt this stagnation in the town's growth. Indeed, it was not until 1851 that Worthing re-emerged as one of England's principal seaside resorts. Resort development was becoming a significant element in the overall economy of Sussex and, as inland agriculture began to decline, profit now lay in the developing coastal resorts. Consequently, there was a distinct shift in the distribution of the population of Sussex away from the inland agricultural dominated parishes to the emerging seaside resorts.

8th century, the family communities of initial settlement had evolved into nucleated villages and hamlets, which survived free of disruption for many centuries.

The impetus for the town's considerable growth was the burgeoning fashion for holidays beside the sea, which have become an established part of British culture. Sussex, with easy access for London's fashionable clientele, had all the prerequisites for the

WORTHING

INTRODUCTION

THE VICTORIAN HOLIDAY

Kelly's Directory of 1895 suggests that the principal Victorian legacy to Sussex was the creation of 'a main dependence... on its bathing towns'. The select watering place, the antidote to lively Brighton and free of trippers, became a particular phenomenon of the Sussex Coastline.

Worthing did not wish to compete with the garish enjoyments of nearby Brighton, and aimed to continue offering quiet seaside pleasures to the increasing number of holidaying middle-class families. The character was intentionally domestic and reflected the Victorian middle-class ideal, which was a solid suburban house with a semicircular drive, a family carriage, several servants and an annual seaside holiday.

Prior to 1845, only the wealthy had the means to visit Worthing. However, the extension of the railway network to the town in the November of that year opened its doors to the masses. Although annual holidays away from home were still beyond the reach of most Victorians, day excursions to the seaside rapidly became a Victorian institution.

Worthing's tranquillity was threatened by a creeping invasion of clerks, shopkeepers and working class excursionists, bringing together on summer weekends all the contrasting lifestyle patterns of an increasingly complex Victorian social structure. Paternalistic employers, Sunday schools and temperance organisations were all eager to give their dependants and members a taste of the pleasures of the seaside. The Victorian virtue of thrift, encouraged by the Christmas club, picnic club and holiday savings club, opened up the seaside to a wide spectrum of the working classes. At first, most of the working classes arrived only for the day, but their very different demeanour posed a direct threat to the secure enjoyment and complacency of the established middle-class Victorian family holiday.

THE VIEW FROM THE PIER 1899 43948

At low tide, buckets and spades sold well as young and old alike built sand castles, while the local fishermen, finding the appeal of pleasure boating stronger than the rigours of fishing, told tales of winter gales and stormy seas to enchanted children.

THE BEACH 1890 22678

The characteristic mid-Victorian, family-orientated, open-air seaside culture, which offered a satisfaction of its own, and the town's secure, peaceful ambience is captured in this view of the beach. Middle-class holidaymakers enjoy the sea air, surrounded by their children, without any distractions or noise from the variety of entertainments found at other South coast resorts. Pebbles now cover the upper part of the formerly sandy beach, described by John Evans in the town's first guidebook, published in 1804, as being 'as smooth as a carpet and level as a lawn'. The ubiquitous deck chair is nowhere to be seen. Most are content to sit either on the pebbles or groynes in their best clothes, while hats and sunshades protect pale, delicate skins from the currently unfashionable suntan.

THE VIEW FROM THE PIER 1903 50078A

At high tide, for the cost of a few shillings, the more adventurous could be wafted along the coast in one of the town's many pleasure boats.

THE VICTORIAN HOLIDAY

Left (Above and Detail):
VIEW FROM THE PIER 1899 43947

Rather than waste time and money
queuing for a bathing machine, most
day trippers paddled about at the
water's edge. They did not undress and
go swimming from the beach until
Edwardian times.

THE VICTORIAN HOLIDAY

THE BEACH 1903 50079

The bathing machines still to be seen in this view of the beach were a remnant of the past, for by 1900 medicinal sea-bathing was in terminal decline.

The Bye-laws regulating public bathing at Worthing still required bathing machines to be segregated by sex, with those for male bathers being located a minimum of 50 yards from those used by female bathers. The ten bathing machines at the water's edge located between Steyne Passage and the west side of Library Place were for female bathers and the sign indicating their location was clearly visible on the Esplanade. It would appear that few if any were being used as most of the visitors were content to either paddle or occupy their time on the beach playing with their children.

It is evident why the use of bathing machines was in terminal decline, for the nearest bathing machines for male bathers were located on the west side of the Pier, between New Street and the west entrance to Parade lodge. Those who wished to bathe together as a family, without the encumbrance of a bathing machine, had to either go beyond Windsor Road in the east or Sea View Road in the west, beyond the view of both visitors and inhabitants alike.

THE VICTORIAN HOLIDAY

THE VIEW FROM THE PIER 1899 43946

Unlike Worthing's early 19th century fashionable clientele and subsequent Victorian middle-class visitors, few of Worthing's late-Victorian day trippers were attracted to the town simply to swim in the sea.

For decades, bathing machines and their notorious attendants aided the ritual of sea-bathing for medicinal purposes. By the beginning of the 19th century, most resorts had a collection of bathing machines for visitors' use; bathing machines were recorded at Worthing from as early as 1789. This room on wheels was dragged into the water by a horse and — in theory — provided all the privacy of an indoor bathing establishment. No lady would have considered bathing without its protective presence. Having reached the water's edge, the reluctant bather was assisted by the dipper. While it often required the effort of two or more stalwart 'longshoremen' to duck the gentlemen bathers, a stout and fantastically garbed old woman usually officiated for the ladies.

As more and more people came to spend their holidays by the sea, pleasure supplanted health as the dominant motive for bathing. Even so, Victoria's reign was well over before respectable women could be seen strolling on the beach in their bathing costumes. Indeed, no middle-class Victorian lady would ever have contemplated paddling in the sea. Only their maids or the children's nannies could do something so undignified. By the beginning of the 20th century, there was growing pressure to allow mixed family bathing, but prudery and vested interest continued to restrict visitors' freedom at most resorts.

This pressure forced coastal local authorities to seek regulatory powers, most involving the use of local bye-laws. The Borough of Worthing Bye-laws with respect to Public Bathing 1892 stated that 'Regulation Costume means a Garment or Combination of Garments extending from the neck to the knees, and being of a thickness, material, shape and otherwise sufficient to effectually prevent indecent exposure of the person of the bather.' The penalty for infringing the Bye-laws was £5.

Sunny Worthing

In the 1920s and 30s, the seaside remained a lively and vibrant place for young people and children. In stark contrast to the late-Victorian era, Worthing became much more relaxed and cosmopolitan. Most visitors still migrated to the beach, many still dressed in their Sunday best. Sun-shades still continued to protect delicate skins from the sun but there were now many more cloth caps and straw bonnets. Even though deck chairs were now readily available, many still chose to sit on either the pebbles or the groynes. Entertainment remained simple and traditional. There were donkey rides at low tide and Punch and Judy, the best known and loved of all the seaside attractions, amused almost as many adults as children.

Between the wars, the family car became a status symbol for many middle class families. By 1920 there were 200,000 cars on the road and by 1938 this number had grown to over 2 million. An increasing number of motorcycles provided the same freedom of movement to the upper working classes. Most visitors, however, still travelled to Worthing by train. The census taken in June 1921 reveals that there were an estimated 3,700 visitors in the town, most of whom lived in either London or the south-east of England. More than 53,000 day trippers visited Worthing on August Bank Holiday 1935 and in 1938 over 80,000 return tickets were booked at Victoria Station in London.

SUNNY WORTHING

THE BEACH 1903 50079

SUNNY WORTHING

Right: THE BEACH 1903 50081

Buckets and spades continued to sell well as children continued to
enjoy making sandcastles on the beach, which had become their
play-ground. Some attempted to catch shrimps with their home-
made nets, while others collected shells and seaweed to take home as
a souvenir of their holiday by the sea.

The ever present band of seaweed deposited by the receding tide
was first recorded at Worthing in 1805, nearly a century before this
photograph was taken. Worthing's Town Commissioners were so
perturbed by its continuing appearance that in December 1828 they
ordered proceedings to be taken against anyone depositing seaweed
in heaps on the beach, apparently under the impression that the
manifestation was the work of some ill-disposed person working
under the cover of darkness!

Left: The catchy advertising slogan 'Sunny Worthing', adopted
by Worthing Borough Council during the first decade of the
20th century, was in stark contrast to the rather pretentious
titles used a decade earlier. In the town's first official guides,
published in the Edwardian period, Worthing was enthusiasti-
cally styled 'The City of Health in the Land of Gardens', 'The
Town of the Vine and Fig' and even the 'English Madeira'.
These titles had been contrived to portray Worthing as a radi-
cally different type of resort and thereby dissuade the lower-
middle and labouring classes from visiting.

CHILDREN ON THE SANDS 1906
56709

Although working class holidays remained unusual before the second decade of the 20th century, most children had been to the seaside on day-trips by the 1930s. Only the luckier ones would have spent a week or more by the sea every summer.

Sunny Worthing

In most resorts bathing had, by the second decade of the 20th century, become a much more relaxed and family centred activity. Swimming was now becoming a recreational activity and this prompted a progressive emancipation in beach attire. Whereas full-skirted and trousered costumes had been the norm at the beginning of the Edwardian period, beach pyjamas and the functional, close-fitting single piece costume were now regularly to be seen.

In the evening visitors were entertained by concert parties at the newly opened Pier Pavilion, watching shows like 'The Colour Box' and 'Gay Parade'. It soon became the centre for Worthing's

THE BEACH 1925 78826

musical entertainment. In 1927 there was a regular quintet, and by 1930 this had expanded to become Worthing's own Municipal Orchestra, which played there every day for the enjoyment of the town's visitors.

Immediately after the Second World War, Worthing, like many other seaside resorts, benefited from an increase in the number of holidaymakers. Throughout the 1950s, the economy of the town was still dependent on an annual influx of visitors. Post-war pictures of the beach show everyone to be much more relaxed (see W147061, pages 26-27). The permanent beach chalets, positioned under a raised sun-terrace, were fully utilised by both local families and visitors. Many were now sunbathing, but the post-war bikini was still conspicuous by its absence. Between May and September 1969, the town attracted an estimated 55,000 staying visitors and 520,000 day visitors. Most were still from the south-east of England, and a large proportion were over 65 years of age.

However, Worthing's era as a leading seaside resort was in terminal decline, with its residential and commercial function finally becoming more predominant.

CARS 1921 71456X

Until the close of the Victorian era, local transport at Worthing was provided solely by horse-bus services. Motor charabanc trips, including long distance journeys, were started in 1907 and were well-established by the 1930s. Most parked adjacent to the pier entrance, advertising their trips and picking up their enthusiastic passengers.

Above: EAST BEACH CHALETS C1955 W147061

Right: MARINE PARADE, C1955 W147015

Surprisingly, by the late 1970s there was strong opposition to any proposal aimed at attracting day-trippers, and the amusements, shops and refreshment facilities used by them were confined to the pier and the adjacent area. As this view of Marine Parade reveals, most of these facilities had taken at least part of their name from the Pier immediately opposite them.

THE ESPLANADE

According to the Wallis Guide Book of 1826, 'Nothing can excel the spectacle that the (Esplanade) presents when thronged, as it is every fine summers' evening, with all the beauty and fashion of the place; while the opportunity it presents for inhaling the ocean breeze in unalloyed purity, and the defence it affords against the sea stamp it with an importance commensurate with its attractive appearance'

Worthing's original promenade had been its sandy beach, but by 1811 this had been superseded by the Steyne, which had been modelled on the recreational area of the same name at Brighton. Ten years later, the Steyne had in turn been superseded by the Esplanade, which immediately became the key rendezvous for late-Georgian visitors.

Prior to its construction, there was only a rough road between the beach and the properties that immediately adjoined the foreshore. There were no sea defences, and during the winter gales the sea often came over the road and flooded the seaward end of the town. When first constructed, the Esplanade only extended from Greville Terrace to West Buildings. It was 20 feet wide and just over half a mile in length, and was the closest that visitors could get to the sea until the pier was constructed in 1862. At night it was lit by a row of handsome lights.

Throughout the Victorian period, social curiosity remained a powerful motivation in the daily life of visitors to the town. Promenading remained an essential part of the resort routine, where everyone came out in their best clothes to both see and be seen. As these photographs reveal, the fashion of promenading, established nearly a century earlier, was perpetuated by both families or individuals, strolling or listening to the bands having become an indispensable part of late-Victorian seaside entertainment.

THE ESPLANADE

THE BANDSTAND 1899 43954

The Esplanade

Western Esplanade and the Beach 1906 56708

THE ESPLANADE

Top: EAST END OF THE ESPLANADE 1890 22710

During the summer of 1894, Oscar Wilde and his family occupied this house overlooking the sea at the eastern end of the extended Esplanade. It was here that he wrote, in the space of only 3 weeks, his most popular play, 'The Importance of Being Earnest' and perhaps as a tribute to the town, named one of the central characters Jack Worthing.

Above: THE BANDSTAND 1921 71452

During the inter-war years, disabled or sick visitors could regularly be seen relaxing in their bath chairs on the Esplanade. This was not a new phenomenon: Worthing's reputation for being especially suitable for such visitors had been established during the 1860s, when an influential doctor estimated that the downs reduced the force of the north winds by about half.

THE ESPLANADE

MARINE PARADE C1955 W147043

By 1867, the Esplanade extended along the entire frontage of both Worthing and West Worthing. In 1930, the western section was improved and extended from Seaview Road to Wallace Avenue. As this post-war picture substantiates, 150 years after its initial construction, the Esplanade remained as popular as ever for promenading by both residents and visitors alike.

THE ESPLANADE

FASHION 1921 71451X

By the end of the Victorian era, women no longer wore bustles, and plain ankle-length skirts became the fashion. Men now wore suits, with jackets and trousers of the same material, but the occasional frock coat was still to be seen. Although men's clothing changed very little in the Edwardian period, women's fashions changed dramatically. Before the First World War, very tight long skirts and large cartwheel hats were fashionable but, as can be seen in this photograph, during the 1920s skirts were loose and much shorter, ending at the knee. Below the cloche hats, pulled low over their eyes, many women wore their hair shorter. In many cases, this represented a conscious decision to turn away from the elaborate clothes and hairstyles of the preceding period, and was an outward sign that women were finally emancipated, able to work and be independent.

THE PIER

THE 'LADY ROWENA' LEAVING THE PIER 1921 71464

As part of Worthing Pier's reconstruction in 1888-89, a new landing stage was provided for use mainly by the paddle-steamer excursions which had been introduced in the 1880s. In the early part of the 20th century, the paddle-steamer 'Worthing Belle' was a regular visitor at Worthing, while this photograph shows the 'Lady Rowena' of Glasgow leaving the landing stage in 1921. Even now, the paddle-steamer Waverley continues to make occasional visits to the pier during the summer months.

T he nine earliest piers around the coast of Britain, built between 1815 and 1860, were basically jetties leading to landing stages for the convenience of passengers using pleasure steamers. The Georgian practice of promenading along the seafront quickly spread to these piers. Eventually the purpose built 'pleasure pier' evolved, consisting of a promenade and landing stage, usually constructed of wood and cast iron. Activities such as fishing and occasional performances by small bands supplemented promenading and the normal use of the landing stage. However, it was the introduction of the railways and the associated technology, combined with the desire of the more affluent Victorians for holidays by the sea, that brought about the construction of some sixty-three piers between 1860 and 1900. By charging a toll for the privilege of promenading and a small fee from boat passengers using the landing stage, piers were viewed as exciting and viable propositions by

prospective Pier Companies.

Worthing's original pier, financed by the Worthing Pier Company, was built in 1862 at a cost of £6,500. A basic iron structure, it was 960 feet long and 16 feet wide with wooden

THE PIER 1921 71444

Worthing Pier enjoyed its heyday in the Edwardian period, when thousands
of visitors flocked to piers for their fun and excitement. However, on Easter
Monday 1913, a violent storm destroyed most of its length between the shore
and the Southern Pavilion. Yet by 1914 the Pier was rebuilt and officially opened
by the Lord Mayor of London. The rebuilt Pier is depicted in this photograph.

decking leading to a platform at the sea end. By the late Victorian period, the majority of piers were very successful and a greater variety of entertainment and comfort was being offered. Concert halls were built on the piers and the bands and musicians, who previously performed in the open air only in suitable weather conditions, could now operate under cover. Consequently in 1888-89, Worthing Pier was widened and a pavilion seating 650 people was built at its seaward end.

THE PIER

ON THE PIER c1955   W147048

THE PIER

The Pier

Pier Entrance 1921 71457

Due to the Pier's popularity and success, improvements were made in
1884 by replacing the tollhouse that originally stood in the centre of
the entrance with two new kiosks. These survived the 1913 storm and
can clearly be seen in this photograph. The western kiosk, shown in the
foreground at the Pier's entrance, was utilised as the tollhouse, while
the other was a bazaar (or 'fancy depository') from which souvenirs
were sold. Many local establishments and events were advertised on the
kiosks over the years and an example can just be seen on the right.

THE PIER

Disaster struck the Pier in September 1933 when a fire destroyed the Southern Pavilion and Pier Head, but within two years it had been redesigned and rebuilt at a cost of £18,000. During the Second World War, the Military Authorities occupied the Pier and, in common with other piers along the south coast, a section of Worthing Pier was blown up to stop enemy troops from landing on it. After the war the Pier was repaired and eventually re-opened in 1949. The Pier and part of the seafront shown in the photograph of circa 1955 (W147048, pages 36-37) is viewed from the Southern Pavilion which, in recent years, has been used as a night-club. The windscreen, down the centre of the Pier, and amusement arcade (the building with clock and flags on top) were erected in 1937. The larger building is the Pier Pavilion at the shore end of the Pier. Today the Pier is still a popular attraction for visitors and admission is free.

THE PIER PAVILION 1925 78818

In 1920, the Corporation purchased the Pier and within six years the two kiosks had been demolished and the imposing Pier Pavilion erected at the Pier entrance. A shop replaced the one in the old kiosk. The Pier Pavilion was designed by the architects Adshead and Ramsey and opened in 1926 to provide a permanent home for music and recreation. By 1930 it had become the centre of Worthing's musical entertainment, with the Municipal Orchestra playing there daily, and various other activities taking place in the summer. The Denton Lounge (now the Café Denton) was added to the western side of the Pavilion and opened in 1959. Wide-ranging entertainment is still provided throughout the year.

THE BANDSTAND

In 1897 W Macfarlane of Glasgow erected an iron 'birdcage' bandstand on the Esplanade, west of the Pier at Worthing. However, by 1907, a long curved shelter had been built between the beach and the bandstand, and the long seats had been replaced by deckchairs for hire. In this year, it was recorded that only visiting bands were performing in the bandstand. Later, a rectangular area around the bandstand and shelter was enclosed with a low fence, as can be seen in the 1921 photograph (71445).

After the First World War the birdcage style became unfashionable and in 1925 the Worthing bandstand was demolished. It was replaced by a spacious band enclosure constructed on steel piling.

It was designed by the architects Adshead and Ramsey and built at a cost of £25,000. The arena was semicircular and over 200 feet in length, with 150 feet extending over the shingle beach. A canopied stage on the southern side faced 800 covered seats around the outside, while the central area offered a further seating capacity of 1,400. The canopied stage was converted to a domed structure in 1929. A decline in demand resulted in the conversion of the bandstand in 1958-9 to an open-air, unheated swimming pool (the Lido) which opened in the summer months only. Thirty years later, after a number of problems and non-profitability, another conversion led to its use as the entertainment centre that still operates today.

THE BANDSTAND AND PARADE 1899
44882

The birdcage bandstand design was very popular at many seaside resorts. At Worthing long movable seats were provided for people enjoying performances by the town band, which had been formed in 1897. Although the concerts appear to have been appreciated by visitors and inhabitants, the bandstand itself did not impress the author of 'The New Hygeia' (a guide to Worthing and its neighbourhood circa 1898). The author noted, 'we come to the Band Stand, a structure which calls for no enthusiastic comment, being more suggestive of a tea garden than of a grand parade'.

THE BANDSTAND

THE BANDSTAND AND PIER 1921 71445

THE BAND ENCLOSURE AND PIER 1925 78824

MARINE PARADE

Immediately behind the Esplanade were Worthing's numerous lodging houses and hotels. Many dated from Worthing's initial development as a fashionable Georgian watering place during the late 18th and early 19th centuries. In all the emerging resorts, the provision of accommodation for visitors had been a high priority, and at Worthing terraces of lodging houses were constructed on the former agricultural land that adjoined the foreshore. Once complete, they were immediately let at exorbitant rents.

Most escaped the extensive demolition that took place between 1950 and 1970, when many of Worthing's important historical buildings were destroyed to satisfy the late 20th century preoccupation with redevelopment. With the exception of the Dome Cinema, all the buildings shown on the 1890 picture of Marine Parade are also shown on the picture taken circa 1965.

MARINE PARADE 1890 22680 (DETAIL)

This tobacconist's shop (far left on above photograph) was originally Murray's English and Foreign Bazaar, which is first shown on Wallis' street map of Worthing dated 1826. By 1890 it had become a tobacconist's shop run by a Mr Goldsmith. In Kelly's directory for 1960 it is still listed as a tobacconist, newsagent and confectioners. Other than the addition of a modern sunblind and signage, nothing had really changed for over 75 years.

Little Terrace (centre on above photograph) was built as a terrace of fashionable lodging houses by a Brighton bricklayer named William Hall circa 1794. It was a typical Regency seaside terrace, built of brick, faced in stucco or painted plaster, with an ironwork balcony that had a curved tiled roof like a Chinese pagoda. When this picture was taken in 1890 it was still a lodging house, but by 1931 it had been converted into the Southdown Restaurant.

By 1894 the two smaller lodging houses, inappropriately named Great Terrace (right on above photograph), had been constructed at the southern end of Bedford Row. These were also lodging houses in 1890, but had become the offices of the Southdown Motor Company by 1931. In 1965 the building was Macari's Ice Cream Parlour.

DETAIL FROM THE DOME CINEMA W147140

Built by C A Seebold in 1909 as a 'Kursaal' in the garden of Bedford House, the Dome Cinema was originally a roller skating rink with a hall for concerts at first floor level. It was converted by Seebold in 1921 into Worthing's first permanent cinema.

MARINE PARADE

During the first two decades of the 19th century, the more affluent of Worthing's Georgian visitors often took over entire houses on a long lease, so that they could cater for themselves and also entertain. In many cases, they brought their own servants with them.

Although Evans suggests in Worthing's first guide book, published in 1805, that 'there was accommodation suitable for every class of visitor', the town still lacked a first-class hotel to satisfy the needs of the increasing number of fashionable visitors. The Steyne Hotel, which opened on 1 July 1807, fulfilled this need as the town's first purpose built hotel.

In 1867 there were only 54 lodging houses in Worthing. By 1891 this had increased to over 200. Visitors, when looking westwards from the pier in 1899, would have seen terrace after terrace of lodging houses, interspersed with the occasional Victorian hotel, stretching to beyond the Heene Parish boundary.

EAST PARADE 1919 68987

The Steyne Hotel (left on above photograph) opened in 1807, when its assembly room immediately became the social centre of the emerging resort. Stafford's New Worthing Guide, published in 1810, reveals that there was an elegant coffee room and handsome sitting rooms on the ground floor, together with private rooms and offices for the household. Over these were the ballroom/assembly room, a card room and other suites of apartments 'in the first degree of elegance'.

THE ESPLANADE 1890 22706

Prior to 1820, the expansion of Worthing had been haphazard. There had been no grandiose schemes comparable, in either size or style, with the squares and crescents that had been created at Hove or Brighton. York Terrace, the imposing building shown in the picture, was built circa 1822 by Edward Evershed. This terrace of five separate lodging houses, with their stucco facades, ionic pilasters, porches and balconies, was without doubt one of Worthing's most impressive Regency buildings.

MARINE PARADE

By the end of the Victorian period the scale of amenities offered by larger boarding houses, such as the Eardley Boarding Establishment at Splash Point, often overlapped with those of newly erected Victorian hotels such as the Clear View which catered for the more affluent visitors. While the development of the railway network brought an ever-increasing number of day-trippers to the seaside, by the late-Victorian period the railway was also conveying an increasing number of middle-class families who stayed in the hotels of the more select resorts.

Unlike Brighton, Eastbourne and Hastings, Worthing never aspired to having an opulent purpose built Victorian hotel. Although plans were passed in 1893 for a 370-room Hotel Metropole and another pier at the western end of the town, the scheme failed. The empty shell of the unfinished hotel at the southern end of Grand Avenue remained empty for years bearing witness to its planned, but failed, viability.

WARNES HOTEL 1925 78821

In 1899, G H Warnes converted York Terrace into Worthing's premier hotel, with a Palm Court sextet performing daily in the ballroom. As a pioneering motorist himself, Warnes recognised the tourist potential of the motor car, and in York Road opened what was claimed to be the first garage incorporated into an English hotel.

STANHOE HALL HOTEL 1899 43957

The building that later became the Stanhoe Hotel was a remnant of the western extremity of the Georgian town. Built in the first decade of the 19th century, it was located at the southern end of Trafalgar Place. Originally named Trafalgar House, it was re-named Augusta House after Princess Augusta, daughter of George III, who stayed there during the winter of 1829-30.

THE CLEAR VIEW HOTEL c1965 W147122

Unlike the Stanhoe Hotel, the Clear View was typical of the small to medium-sized hotels that had been built on the former open spaces and lawns of the Georgian resort. Its site had formerly been the lawn to Summer Lodge, which was offered by its owner Miles Stringer to Princess Amelia during her brief visit in 1798, so that she was able to sit in the fresh air when the state of the tide prevented her from being carried to the beach. Its name was very apt, for like all the hotels and boarding houses in Marine Parade, its upper rooms and balconies had an unimpeded view of the English Channel.

THE EARDLEY HOTEL c1965 W147105

In 1890, the building that became the Eardley Hotel shown here was still the Eardley House Boarding Establishment, run by a Miss Butler. Few respectable occupations were open to the legion of unattached Victorian women from the less affluent levels of the middle classes. Lodging house keeping was particularly attractive, as in many cases it provided an income sufficient to maintain a single women in the style to which she aspired.

Marine Parade

Marine Parade

MARINE PARADE

During the 1920s and 30s, Worthing continued to rapidly expand. By 1937 the town was being promoted as both a summer and winter resort, and hotels now occupied much of the sea front and the area behind it.

The Beach Hotel had opened at 4 Marine Parade in 1915, expanding into the whole parade by 1936, when the original red-brick houses that had, in part, comprised The Prince Albert Convalescent Home were remodelled in cement Deco-style.

Many of the Victorian boarding houses had been converted into hotels, and most of the modern hotels illustrated date from this period, albeit trading under different names.

Although Worthing initially benefited from an increase in the number of holidaymakers after the Second World War, the town continued to lack any large hotels. By the early 1970s, Worthing, like most English seaside resorts, was having to compete with package holidays abroad. Many of the town's hotels tried to fill their rooms by becoming conference venues.

Right, Top to Bottom
THE PRINCE ALBERT CONVALESCENT HOME AND THE BEACH HOTEL 1919 68986

THE BEACH HOTEL C1965 W147144

THE CUMBERLAND HOTEL C1965 W147151

PRINCES TERRACE, MARINE PARADE 1921 71460

Far Right, Top to Bottom:
THE CAVENDISH HOTEL C1965 W147110

THE GRANVILLE HOTEL C1960 W147121

VIEW FROM WEST PARADE 1919 68983

This hotel opened in c1839 as the King and Queen, offering accommodation for early-Victorian visitors to the town. By 1874 it had become the Brunswick Hotel.

THE KINGSWAY HOTEL C1955 W147114

Prior to the construction of Princess Terrace between Queens Road and Thorn Road, this site had been used as a sand-pit by the Parish of Heene to provide employment for the poor during the winter months. By 1930 many of the boarding houses had become small family run hotels and the Kingsway Hotel had opened at the eastern end.

Left: MARINE PARADE C1955 W147043

MARINE PARADE

Marine Parade

MARINE PARADE

VIEW FROM WEST PARADE 1919 68983

THE TOWN CENTRE

Prior to the 19th century, South Street was part of old Worthing Street, which wound its way down through Worthing to the sea. The latter part of this route is now modern High Street, Warwick Street and South Street. Worthing became a town in 1803 but during the transitional period from circa 1790, Worthing Street was divided into several pieces and each piece renamed — some of them more than once! At the end of the 18th century, South Street was referred to as West Lane. Phillip's map of Worthing in 1814 shows that the whole of South Street was developed, with the exception of the stretch between Montague Street and Liverpool Road. Development of this part did not commence until after 1866. After circa 1860 the area around South Street, the eastern end of Montague Street and the pier became the entertainment centre of the town. At the northern end of South Street was the Town Hall and Warwick Street, which led in an easterly direction towards High Street and Steyne Gardens (see photograph, and map, page 56).

Between 1803 and 1808 substantial and fashionable residential buildings were erected on the north side of Warwick Street on land formerly used for agriculture. Most of the buildings had bow windows and steps leading up to elegant doorways which, sadly, have now all been replaced by modern shop fronts. However, above these a few of the bow windows still remain.

On the south side of Warwick Street were old buildings, several of which had to be demolished before substantial development could take place. Worthing's first two banks were built on this side of the street but, unfortunately, have not survived. One of the very few preserved buildings in this vicinity is Stanford's Cottage, situated in a small area developed as Stanford Square in 1985. Stanford's Cottage is currently Grade II listed and used as a restaurant.

SOUTH STREET 1895 35075

A branch of the London and County Banking Company Limited was established between 1845 and 1849 at 4 South Street. In 1881 it was one of only two banks in Worthing, the other being Henty's Bank in Warwick Street. Records show that in 1890, the branch was sited at 41 and 43 South Street, opposite the Town Hall, at the opposite end and side of the street. By 1891 it had been moved to 17 South Street (as shown in this photograph) where it remained for many years. The horse and cart visible outside the building belonged to the butcher, Mr C Archer, whose shop was next door at number 15. Near the cart can be seen a small penny-farthing cycle leaning against the lamp-post.

WORTHING

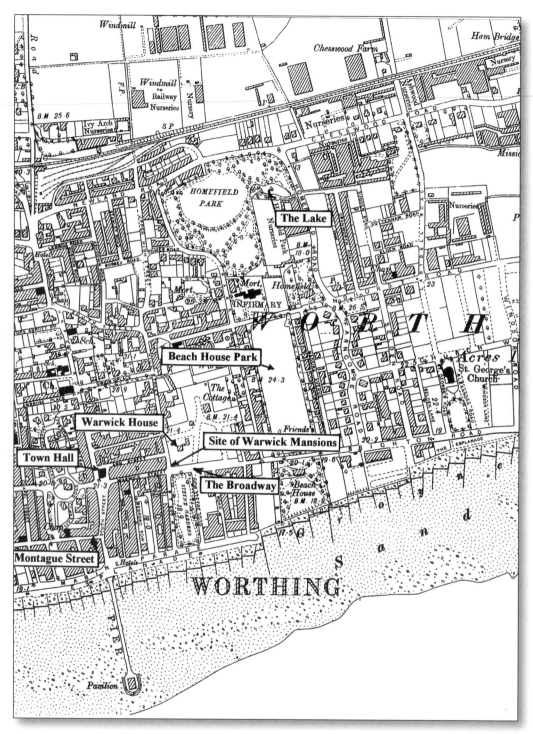

ORDNANCE SURVEY MAP OF CENTRAL WORTHING 1898

The buildings on the corner of High Street and The Broadway were named Warwick Mansions. This commemorated the fact that in 1901, they were erected on the site of old Warwick House, which had been demolished a few years earlier. The trees and flint wall in the photograph marked the southern boundary of the Warwick estate. These were retained as a feature when part of the Brighton Road was widened on either side and renamed The Broadway. A Worthing Directory for 1919 records the three visible shops at ground level (on the left of photograph 68989) as Colin Moore, a perambulator depot (behind the balustrade), Ivens, Kelletts and Childs, chemists and F C Whittington, bootmaker. Although the buildings remain virtually unchanged today, the trees and wall were removed in 1928.

SOUTH STREET 1899 43956

An 1821 Act of Parliament specified financial limits within which Worthing Town Commissioners could purchase land to erect a building to hold their meetings and provide and maintain a town clock. A Town Hall with a clock was built at a cost of £1,215 8s 10d on land at the northern end of South Street and opened without ceremony in 1835. Beneath the building were cells for accommodating prisoners and a space for housing the hand-operated fire engine and ladder that were gifts to the town. The Incorporation Ceremony of the Borough of Worthing was conducted from its steps on 3 September 1890. Although it remained the focal point of municipal administration for many years, it was finally replaced in 1933 by a Town Hall built further to the north in Chapel Road. The old Town Hall building was finally demolished in 1966 and its site covered by the entrance to the modern Guildbourne shopping precinct.

THE TOWN CENTRE

FROM THE AIR

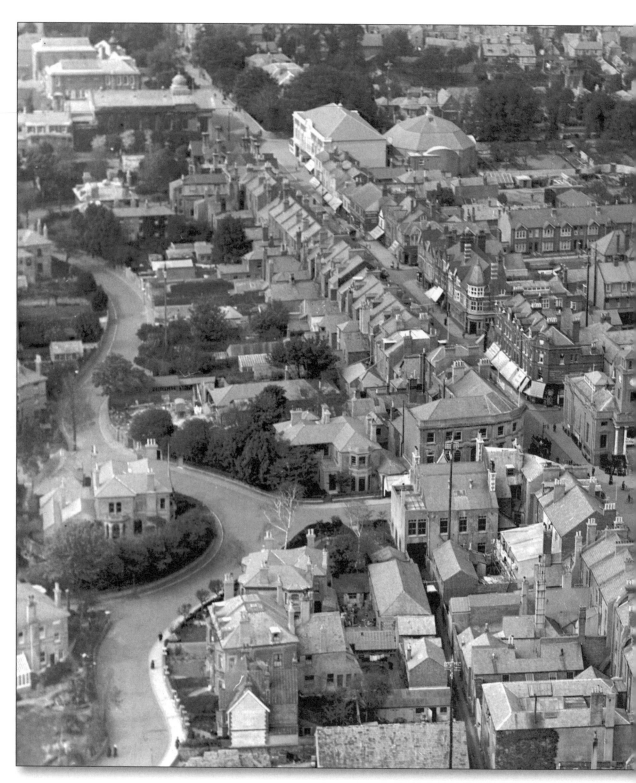

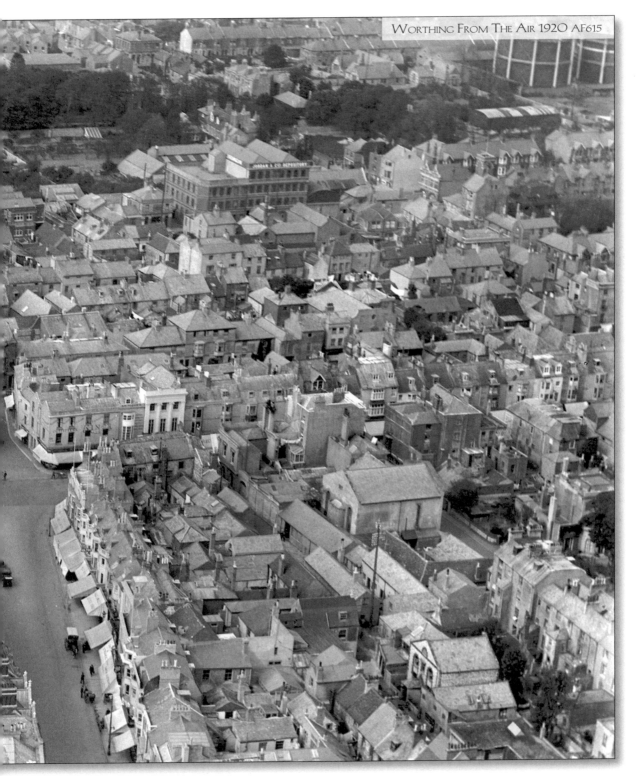

RECREATIONAL FACILITIES

As social curiosity remained a powerful motivation in the visitor's daily life during the late Victorian period, most resorts provided as many gathering places as they could afford. Worthing's first park was opened in 1881 on approximately fourteen acres of land which had been given to the town by three of its prominent citizens. The park was known variously as the Peoples' Park, The Park and later Homefield Park (its site being located on the former open or common field known as the Home Field prior to enclosure). It was laid out with tree-lined walks, seats and an attractive lake fed by the Teville stream. Kirshaw's 'Guide and Handbook to Worthing and its vicinity', published in 1883, describes the recreational scene: 'A wall surrounds the Park in which a cricket ground has been laid out. Trees have been planted, and walks made, one of which leads to an ornamental lake, which is prettily situated, and with its grassed banks and artificial 'islands' forms a picturesque spot. That the Park will prove a boon to the inhabitants and visitors is beyond doubt, but some years may elapse before its advantages will be fully appreciated'.

In 1887 the Park was enlarged, and nurseries were sited south-east of the lake by the 1890s.

THE PARK 1892 29965

THE PARK 1906 56714

...06 56715

...d the lake was very popular with
...Edwardian families, and many picturesque
...produced, often showing children look-
...d feeding the swans on the lake. Two of these
...graphs, of an almost identical view but taken 14
...rs apart, show how the Park's earlier plain appearance
...matured into a very pleasant Edwardian lakeside scene.
Regrettably, the lake was removed in 1934 and its site
grassed over. The nurseries have also gone and the area
has been developed as part of Park Avenue.

RECREATIONAL FACILI

It was during the latter part of Queen Victoria's reign that sport and recreation quickly spread to the working classes. Large numbers, now employed in industrial and other services or tasks, were no longer tied to the relentless agricultural pursuits of their forefathers. Additionally, the town was growing: Worthing and Heene were incorporated by charter in 1890 as the Borough of Worthing and the town's boundaries were extended to encompass a total of 1,425 acres.

Exercise through sport was perceived as beneficial and by the 1890s Worthing had clubs for cricket, association and rugby football,

B
Club
bowls we

When fur
parishes of Broad
almost doubled to
impetus to the increas
and 1901 when the popul
to 16,606. By 1911, the popu

30,308. At this time, the town's additional open spaces were Steyne Gardens (near the pier), which had been acquired in 1900, and the Victoria Recreation Ground, which opened in 1901 and was catering mainly for the Heene and West Tarring area.

The borough's need for additional outdoor facilities was at its greatest during the inter-war period. The borough boundaries were extended in 1929 to take in neighbouring Goring and Durrington, the remainder of Broadwater and West Tarring; the resulting area was referred to as Greater Worthing. Later boundary extensions took in parts of Findon and Sompting.

The combined effect of these boundary changes effectively trebled the area of the borough to just over 8,000 acres. Between the years 1921 and 1941 the population more than doubled from approximately 30,000 to 62,000, due not only to the borough's extended boundaries but also to the town's rapid expansion during the 1920s and 1930s when new residents became commuters to Brighton and London. Further impetus was given by the electrification of the railway line between West Worthing and London, which also increased the number of visitors to the town.

The Bowling Green in The Park 1906 56716

Today it is recognised that Worthing's premier sport is bowls. Prior to 1924, the only bowling green in the town was at Homefield Park (formerly The Park), this being home to the Worthing Bowling Club with its sixty members. After two further bowling greens were made available to the public at Beach House park in 1924, Worthing Bowling Club moved there and a Homefield Park Bowling Club was formed to play on the vacant green. Over the years, interest in the game has undoubtedly been influenced by the town's attraction for the elderly and retired who come to live here permanently. In 1901, just over 10% of the town's population were aged 60 or over, this being 3% higher than the average for England and Wales. In 1931 this percentage was recorded as 14%; however, the age group had been adjusted to take in people aged 65 or over.

RECREATIONAL FACILITIES

MARINE PARADE C1955 W147037

Roller-skating was first recorded in Worthing in the last quarter of the 19th century. In circa 1910, at least three rinks existed, including one at the end of the Pier and another in the Kursaal, which opened that year. During the First World War, the Germanic-sounding name Kursaal was changed to The Dome. In 1921 the skating rink was converted into Worthing's first permanent cinema.

RECREATIONAL FACILITIES

The Corporation's policy of providing a sufficient number of public parks and recreation grounds for both residents and visitors was actively pursued during this period of expansion. In excess of fifteen additional areas for outdoor recreation were provided and by 1938 there were seven separate recreation grounds (amounting to fifty acres) and ten public parks recorded in the borough. Several of these combine formal gardens and walks with sports facilities.

During the 1930s two additional bowling greens were laid out at separate locations within the borough, one at Marine Gardens in 1930 (see W147157) and one at Church House Grounds in 1937. Marine Gardens, a small park located in West Parade between Grand Avenue and Wallace Avenue, was laid out on two and a half acres of land in 1930 and contains ornamental gardens (see W147146), a pavilion, one putting green and one bowling green. Over the years it has maintained its popularity and is still well attended.

RECREATIONAL FACILITIES

Right and Above:
BOWLING GREENS, BEACH HOUSE PARK c1955
W147025

In 1922, the Corporation purchased Beach House Park, which was originally ten acres of enclosed meadow surrounded by trees. It was laid out with tennis courts and two bowling greens and opened in 1924. An additional green was opened in 1926 and another in 1934. By 1938, Worthing was a recognised bowls centre, with its Annual Bowls Tournament being held at Beach House Park. This was very popular and was considered to be one of the most important held in the country. By 1951, the percentage of Worthing residents aged over 65 had risen to 25%, while by 1971, this figure had risen again to 34% — over two and half times the average for England and Wales. Correspondingly, the popularity of bowls in Worthing increased and a fifth bowling green was added to Beach House Park in 1967. In 1972 the Second World Bowls Championships were held there. The reputation of Beach House Park as a bowls centre was further enhanced in 1988 when the English Bowls Association built their headquarters there. In 1992, it became the venue for the Woolwich World Bowls Championships with twenty-eight competing countries.

Right:

BEACH HOUSE PARK c1965 W147138

Although Beach House Park is renowned for its bowling greens and tournaments it also contains ornamental gardens, grass areas and walks at its southern end. This photograph shows a bed planted with flowers, small shrubs and trees, situated not far from the main gates. Paths lead to the centre of the bed where there is an unusual memorial to 'Warrior Birds who gave their lives on active service during 1939-45 and for the use and pleasure of living birds'. It was presented by the actress and producer Nancy Price and members of the Peoples' Theatre, London.

RECREATIONAL FACILITIES

Beach House Park and the house and grounds opposite (between the Brighton Road and the beach) were originally part of the same privately owned estate. The appropriately named house was built in 1820. The grounds of the house contained many forest and ornamental trees. There was a rose garden, walled kitchen garden, greenhouse and a large lawn. King Edward VII visited Beach House on several occasions between 1907 and 1910 when it belonged to Sir Edmund Loder.

By 1927 the Corporation had purchased Beach House and its grounds on the southern side of Brighton Road. In 1937-38 the boating and paddling pools were laid out on the eastern side of these grounds. Although adjacent to the sea, the paddling pool was

THE PADDLING POOL c1955 W147028

a convenient alternative for children at high tide, when the sea was too rough or the seawater temperature unacceptable. During the 1950s and 60s the two pools were very popular, as can be seen in the photographs.

To the right of the photograph of the Boating Pool (W147031, pages 72-73), a building can just be seen amongst the trees above the changing rooms: this was originally Worthing College. It became a convalescent home, later known as Beachfield, which was converted to flats prior to its demolition in 1967. The Aquarena Swimming Complex which was then built on the site opened in 1968, providing a wide range of wet and dry recreational activities. It has since proved to be one of Worthing's most popular facilities.

Recreational Facilities

CHILDREN'S BOATING POOL c1955 W147031

RECREATIONAL FACILITIES

EAST BEACH CHALETS C1955 W147032

The remainder of Beach House grounds to the west of the boating and paddling pools was also laid out in 1937-38. It included tennis courts and a grassed area that stretched from Beach House to the old estate's southern boundary. A row of forty-eight beach chalets was also constructed facing the sea. In front of the row was a sun terrace, while close to each end there was a brick tower-like structure. As can be seen in the photograph above, one of these towers is topped with a clock: a plaque reads 'Festival of Britain, 1951. The above clock was given by war-time children and accepted on behalf of the Borough by the Mayor Cr. Mrs Rita Esme Summers, J.P.' A promenade was constructed between these towers that ran along the top of the chalets, with steps at either end. Between the sun terrace and the shingle beach, another walkway was provided at ground level. This effectively made the esplanade continuous to the Brighton Road on the east. Both promenades have remained popular over the years with residents and visitors, not only in the summer months but

74

THE VIEW FROM DENTON GARDENS C1965 W147136

Denton Gardens was named after Alderman J G Denton who presented it to the town in June 1922. It is a small park laid out on two acres of land and contains two 18 hole putting courses, a raised terrace with shelters facing the sea and the park and a sunken garden with a lily pond. It was opened to the public in the spring of 1924. The wall in which this archway is constructed separates the Gardens from the western side of Beach House grounds. Peter Pan's Playground can be seen from ground level.

also with those who wish to experience invigorating walks by the sea during the sometimes less inviting off-season weather. The playground, which can be seen just beyond the raised promenade on the left, was constructed in Beach House grounds and opened in 1951 as Peter Pan's Playground. The entrance is just below the white notice-board by the mock fort. Among the original items of play equipment were the fort, a helter-skelter, slides and swings. Unsurprisingly, this playground was a great attraction for children.

For many centuries Worthing, part of the ancient ecclesiastical parish of Broadwater, did not possess a church of its own. The Domesday Survey reveals there was a church at Broadwater in 1086 and, although no part of the structure is still visible, a church is thought to have existed here in Saxon times. The present church at Broadwater was commenced some time after 1100 and is one of the largest cruciform churches in Sussex.

Worthing's first church was St Paul's in Chapel Road. It was opened for divine worship in 1812 as a 'proprietary chapel of ease' to Broadwater, to accommodate the increasing number of fashionable visitors to the town. The building costs were paid by subscription. Money to maintain this church and pay the incumbent, known as the Chaplain, was raised by the sale and leasing of pews, and a rate was levied on the pews' proprietors. Not surprisingly most of these proprietors were the landlords of the lodgings and furnished houses in the town.

The church of St George (pages 80-81) was consecrated in 1868, apparently to serve the development on the eastern side of the expanding town. It appears, however, that this church had been built for potential rather than actual worshippers, for the surrounding land remained market gardens and was not built on until 1909.

St Paul's Church 1906 56713

St Paul's Church was designed by J B Rebecca in the Greek style and was constructed with yellow bricks made locally from the blue clay to be found on the now submerged Worthing Common or Saltgrass. Its eastern end is stuccoed with a bold Doric portico supported on four columns, surmounted by a squat bell-cupola. When originally erected, the chancel was at the eastern end, and there were galleries on all sides. Immediately prior to becoming a parish church in 1894, St Paul's was enlarged and the altar was placed at the western end in a Baroque style chancel.

WORTHING'S CHURCHES

The question of taste was fundamental to Victorian church building. Classic was denounced as vulgar and pagan. The only true style for Christian architecture was pure Gothic, preferably that of the 13th and 14th centuries. St George's, built in flint and stone to a design by George Trufitt, displays an original use of the Gothic style.

At first there was only an apsidal chancel and nave and a singular bell turret. A new vestry and two new porches were added in 1875. By 1884, a transept had also been added.

Between 1873 and 1879 a new Church was built to serve the parish of Heene. Funded by subscriptions as part of West Worthing New Town, the new modern spacious 19th century church of St Botolph's was built near the site of an earlier chapel which had, by the 17th century, fallen into disrepair. By 1778 most of the fabric had been removed, and only a fragment remains, just beyond the eastern end of the new church.

St Andrew's, Clifton Road, was the last parish church to be built in pre-war Worthing. It was possibly also the most controversial, for it marked the beginning of Anglo-Catholicism in the town. One of the underlying factors in the Gothic revival within the Church of England had been the movement towards greater decency and ritual in church services. This began in the 1820s and 1830s among a small group of Oxford dons, and was initially a purely theological aspiration aimed at restoring a greater awareness of the historical church and its hierarchical ministry. By the 1860s there were Anglican churches in both London and the fashionable seaside resorts, where the use of lighted candles, ornate vestments and incense had been revived.

BROADWATER CHURCH 1890 22700

St Mary's Church at Broadwater is constructed in flint rubble with dressings of Caen stone, sandstone and Bath stone and has an impressive Norman tower nearly 140 feet high. On the south side of the church are two crudely made crosses in flint, said to be the only examples of their kind in West Sussex. It originally had a spire but this was removed in 1826 when the south transept chapels were demolished. By circa 1830 the tower had been crenellated. Monuments include two 16th century tombs to the De La Warr family of Offington Hall.

St George's Church 1890 22704

HEENE CHURCH 1894 33768

St Botolph's Church, Heene, was designed by the Brighton architect E C Sott in the Early English style. It was constructed in brick and flint on land donated by the Heene Estate Co. When first erected it consisted of a nave, chancel, north and south aisles with south transept, west tower and spire.

Although the Gothic style flint and Bath stone cruciform church was completed in 1886, it was not consecrated until 1888 due to strong and often bitter opposition from the rector of Broadwater and the vicars of Christchurch and Holy Trinity. Worthing's religious development had, during the 19th century, been profoundly influenced by the evangelical nature of worship at St Mary's Broadwater, and with the exception of Heene, all the churches in the town were strongly evangelical. Most Worthing churches smelt of polished floors and woodwork, rather than incense!

St Andrew's still retains its High Church character and the congregation includes many non-parishioners who prefer the ritualistic style of worship. Meanwhile, the old Chapel of Ease, now St. Paul's, gradually returned from extreme evangelicalism to the middle ground before being closed a few years ago, due to the building fabric having become dangerous.

Although some non-conformists were reluctant, all denominations gradually accepted the Gothic revival. The Baptist Chapel in Christchurch Road, built in brick and flint, reflected this style and was opened for divine worship on 18 March 1885.

ST ANDREW'S CHURCH 1890 22702

Designed by Sir A W Blomfield, St Andrew's Church was built mainly at the expense of its treasurer George Wedd, who also donated the site. It consists of a nave with baptistery, aisles, transepts and Lady Chapel, sacristy and vestry. Internally it has many elaborate furnishings with stained glass and reredos by C E Kempe.

THE BAPTIST CHAPEL 1890 22705

Worthing's first Baptist services took place in a Temperance Hall in
Ann Street in January 1878, and were led by W Stead, a student of the
Pastor's College (today known as Spurgeon's College). Soon after, meetings took place in Montague Hall in Montague Street, where a church
of twenty members was formed with W Stead as its first minister. In
1881 a Particular Baptist chapel was opened in Christchurch Road and
this was registered for worship in 1883. This chapel was replaced in
1885 by the church which had been designed by Resta W Moore.

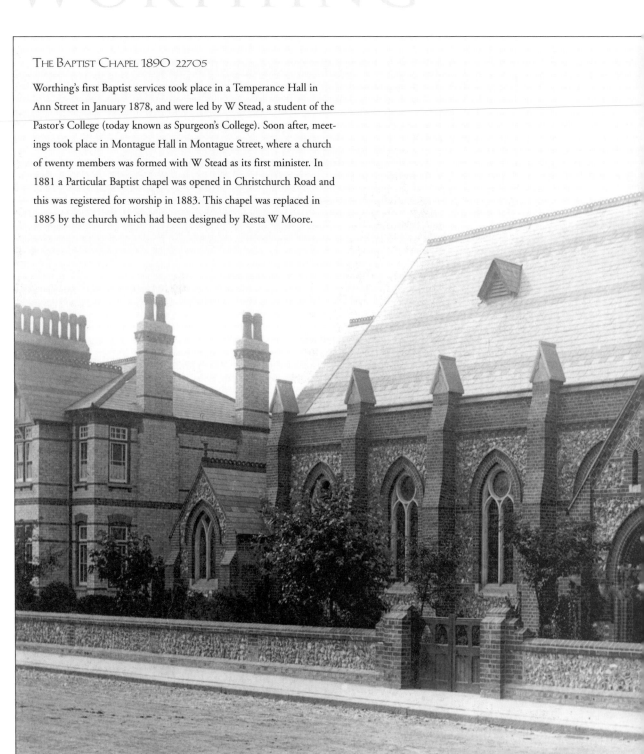

Names of Subscribers

FRANCIS FRITH'S
TOWN&CITY
MEMORIES

The following people have kindly supported this book by purchasing limited edition copies prior to publication.

Gordon C Ashton, Worthing

Mr A W Aves and Mrs C L Aves

David and Dawn Binstead

Edwin Arthur Binstead

Rhoda May Binstead

Martyn and Barbara Booker, Worthing

Rosemary and Gerald Broadwater

The Burrows Family, Worthing

Gwendoline Coxon, Worthing

In memory of Ron Denyer from his family

A Dyson; In memory of E Dyson, Worthing

Mr T C and Mrs J M Edwards, Worthing

For Veronica and The Elliott Family

Mr N P and Mrs K M Franklin

K and N Franklin, for 25 years together, from Sue

The Inglis-Taylors and The Frouds, Worthing

The Furse Family, Worthing

Nanny Iris Harvey, love Jason and Family

For Frank from Helen

In memory of my Nan, E Hillier, Worthing

Dennis Jarvis and Family

To Trevor Jones on his 50th birthday

The Locke Family

Mr A G and Mrs C A Marshall

The Robert Minchin Family

The Murphy Family, Worthing

Allyson, Ben, Natalie, Ralph and Ted Page

The Reynolds Family, Billingshurst

To Richard Russell on your 60th, love from Francis

John and Fay Searle and Family, 1975 to 2005

Brett Searle, a present from Dad, X'mas 2005

Gavin Searle, a present from Dad, X'mas 2005

Wayne Searle, a present from Dad, X'mas 2005

David M Smart, Worthing

The Smith Family, Broadwater

Sydney Charles Stanford on his birthday, love from Pam

The Tapp Family, Worthing

In memory of Don and Ellen Tellick

M J Tingley, related to the Carter Family

Kiran, Jack, Emma and Stephen Wallace

Mr A K Wallis and Mrs J G Wallis, Worthing

Jeannette Wishart

The Worsfold Family

Diana Worsfold

Wicks for my grandchildren, love Yaiyai

INDEX

FRANCIS FRITH'S
TOWN & CITY
MEMORIES

The Francis Frith Collection Titles

www.francisfrith.co.uk

The Francis Frith Collection publishes over 100 new titles each year. A selection of those currently available is listed below. For latest catalogue please contact The Francis Frith Collection. **Town Books** 96 pages, approximately 75 photos. **County and Themed Books** 128 pages, approximately 135 photos (unless specified).

Accrington Old and New
Alderley Edge and Wilmslow
Amersham, Chesham and Rickmansworth
Andover
Around Abergavenny
Around Alton
Aylesbury
Barnstaple
Bedford
Bedfordshire
Berkshire Living Memories
Berkshire Pocket Album
Blackpool Pocket Album
Bognor Regis
Bournemouth
Bradford
Bridgend
Bridport
Brighton and Hove
Bristol
Buckinghamshire
Calne Living Memories
Camberley Pocket Album
Canterbury Cathedral
Cardiff Old and New
Chatham and the Medway Towns
Chelmsford
Chepstow Then and Now
Cheshire
Cheshire Living Memories
Chester
Chesterfield
Chigwell
Christchurch
Churches of East Cornwall
Clevedon
Clitheroe
Corby Living Memories
Cornish Coast
Cornwall Living Memories
Cotswold Living Memories
Cotswold Pocket Album
Coulsdon, Chipstead and Woodmanstern
County Durham
Cromer, Sheringham and Holt
Dartmoor Pocket Album
Derby
Derbyshire
Derbyshire Living Memories
Devon
Devon Churches
Dorchester

Dorset Coast Pocket Album
Dorset Living Memories
Dorset Villages
Down the Dart
Down the Severn
Down the Thames
Dunmow, Thaxted and Finchingfield
Durham
East Anglia Pocket Album
East Devon
East Grinstead
Edinburgh
Ely and The Fens
Essex Pocket Album
Essex Second Selection
Essex: The London Boroughs
Exeter
Exmoor
Falmouth
Farnborough, Fleet and Aldershot
Folkestone
Frome
Furness and Cartmel Peninsulas
Glamorgan
Glasgow
Glastonbury
Gloucester
Gloucestershire
Greater Manchester
Guildford
Hailsham
Hampshire
Harrogate
Hastings and Bexhill
Haywards Heath Living Memories
Heads of the Valleys
Heart of Lancashire Pocket Album
Helston
Herefordshire
Horsham
Humberside Pocket Album
Huntingdon, St Neots and St Ives
Hythe, Romney Marsh and Ashford
Ilfracombe
Ipswich Pocket Album
Isle of Wight
Isle of Wight Living Memories
King's Lynn
Kingston upon Thames
Lake District Pocket Album
Lancashire Living Memories
Lancashire Villages

Available from your local bookshop or from the publisher

The Francis Frith Collection Titles (continued)

Lancaster, Morecambe and Heysham Pocket Album
Leeds Pocket Album
Leicester
Leicestershire
Lincolnshire Living Memoires
Lincolnshire Pocket Album
Liverpool and Merseyside
London Pocket Album
Ludlow
Maidenhead
Maidstone
Malmesbury
Manchester Pocket Album
Marlborough
Matlock
Merseyside Living Memories
Nantwich and Crewe
New Forest
Newbury Living Memories
Newquay to St Ives
North Devon Living Memories
North London
North Wales
North Yorkshire
Northamptonshire
Northumberland
Northwich
Nottingham
Nottinghamshire Pocket Album
Oakham
Odiham Then and Now
Oxford Pocket Album
Oxfordshire
Padstow
Pembrokeshire
Penzance
Petersfield Then and Now
Plymouth
Poole and Sandbanks
Preston Pocket Album
Ramsgate Old and New
Reading Pocket Album
Redditch Living Memories
Redhill to Reigate
Richmond
Ringwood
Rochdale
Romford Pocket Album
Salisbury Pocket Album
Scotland
Scottish Castles
Sevenoaks and Tonbridge
Sheffield and South Yorkshire Pocket Album
Shropshire
Somerset
South Devon Coast
South Devon Living Memories
South East London
Southampton Pocket Album
Southend Pocket Album
Southport

Southwold to Aldeburgh
Stourbridge Living Memories
Stratford upon Avon
Stroud
Suffolk
Suffolk Pocket Album
Surrey Living Memories
Sussex
Sutton
Swanage and Purbeck
Swansea Pocket Album
Swindon Living Memories
Taunton
Teignmouth
Tenby and Saundersfoot
Tiverton
Torbay
Truro
Uppingham
Villages of Kent
Villages of Surrey
Villages of Sussex Pocket Album
Wakefield and the Five Towns Living Memories
Warrington
Warwick
Warwickshire Pocket Album
Wellingborough Living Memories
Wells
Welsh Castles
West Midlands Pocket Album
West Wiltshire Towns
West Yorkshire
Weston-super-Mare
Weymouth
Widnes and Runcorn
Wiltshire Churches
Wiltshire Living Memories
Wiltshire Pocket Album
Wimborne
Winchester Pocket Album
Windermere
Windsor
Wirral
Wokingham and Bracknell
Woodbridge
Worcester
Worcestershire
Worcestershire Living Memories
Wyre Forest
York Pocket Album
Yorkshire
Yorkshire Coastal Memories
Yorkshire Dales
Yorkshire Revisited

See Frith books on the internet at www.francisfrith.co.uk

FRITH PRODUCTS & SERVICES

Francis Frith would doubtless be pleased to know that the pioneering publishing venture he started in 1860 still continues today. Over a hundred and forty years later, The Francis Frith Collection continues in the same innovative tradition and is now one of the foremost publishers of vintage photographs in the world. Some of the current activities include:

Interior Decoration

Today Frith's photographs can be seen framed and as giant wall murals in thousands of pubs, restaurants, hotels, banks, retail stores and other public buildings throughout the country. In every case they enhance the unique local atmosphere of the places they depict and provide reminders of gentler days in an increasingly busy and frenetic world.

Product Promotions

Frith products are used by many major companies to promote the sales of their own products or to reinforce their own history and heritage. Frith promotions have been used by Hovis bread, Courage beers, Scots Porage Oats, Colman's mustard, Cadbury's foods, Mellow Birds coffee, Dunhill pipe tobacco, Guinness, and Bulmer's Cider.

Genealogy and Family History

As the interest in family history and roots grows world-wide, more and more people are turning to Frith's photographs of Great Britain for images of the towns, villages and streets where their ancestors lived; and, of course, photographs of the churches and chapels where their ancestors were christened, married and buried are an essential part of every genealogy tree and family album.

Frith Products

All Frith photographs are available Framed or just as Mounted Prints and Posters (size 23 x 16 inches). These may be ordered from the address below. From time to time other products - Address Books, Calendars, Table Mats, etc - are available.

The Internet

Already ninety thousand Frith photographs can be viewed and purchased on the internet through the Frith websites and a myriad of partner sites.

For more detailed information on Frith companies and products, look at these sites:

www.francisfrith.co.uk
www.francisfrith.com
(for North American visitors)

See the complete list of Frith Books at:
www.francisfrith.co.uk
This web site is regularly updated with the latest list of publications from The Francis Frith Collection. If you wish to buy books relating to another part of the country that your local bookshop does not stock, you may purchase on-line.

For further information, trade, or author enquiries please contact us at the address below:
The Francis Frith Collection, Frith's Barn, Teffont, Salisbury, Wiltshire, England SP3 5QP.
Tel: +44 (0)1722 716 376 Fax: +44 (0)1722 716 881 Email: sales@francisfrith.co.uk

See Frith books on the internet at www.francisfrith.co.uk

FREE PRINT OF YOUR CHOICE

Mounted Print
Overall size 14 x 11 inches (355 x 280mm)

Choose any Frith photograph in this book.
Simply complete the Voucher opposite and
return it with your remittance for £2.25 (to cover
postage and handling) and we will print the
photograph of your choice in SEPIA (size 11 x
8 inches) and supply it in a cream mount with a
burgundy rule line (overall size 14 x 11 inches).
**Please note: photographs with a reference
number starting with a "Z" are not Frith
photographs and cannot be supplied under
this offer.**
Offer valid for delivery to one UK address only.

**PLUS: Order additional Mounted Prints
at HALF PRICE - £7.49 each** (normally £14.99)
If you would like to order more Frith prints from
this book, possibly as gifts for friends and family,
you can buy them at half price (with no
additional postage and handling costs).

PLUS: Have your Mounted Prints framed
For an extra £14.95 per print you can have your
mounted print(s) framed in an elegant polished wood and gilt moulding, overall size 16 x
13 inches (no additional postage and handling
required).

IMPORTANT!

**These special prices are only available if you use
this form to order . You must use the ORIGINAL
VOUCHER on this page (no copies permitted). We
can only despatch to one UK address. This offer
cannot be combined with any other offer.**

Send completed Voucher form to:
**The Francis Frith Collection, Frith's Barn,
Teffont, Salisbury, Wiltshire SP3 5QP**

CHOOSE A PHOTOGRAPH FROM THIS BOOK

Voucher for **FREE** and Reduced Price *Frith Prints*

*Please do not photocopy this voucher. Only the original is valid,
so please fill it in, cut it out and return it to us with your order.*

Picture ref no	Page no	Qty	Mounted @ £7.49	Framed + £14.95	Total Cost £
		1	Free of charge*	£	£
			£7.49	£	£
			£7.49	£	£
			£7.49	£	£
			£7.49	£	£
			£7.49	£	£

*Please allow 28 days
for delivery.
Offer available to one
UK address only*

* Post & handling	£2.25
Total Order Cost	£

Title of this book . . . .

I enclose a cheque/postal order for £ . . . .
made payable to 'The Francis Frith Collection'

OR please debit my Mastercard / Visa / Maestro card,
details below

Card Number

Issue No (Maestro only)   Valid from (Maestro)

Expires   Signature

Name Mr/Mrs/Ms . . . .

Address . . . .

. . . .

. . . .

. . . . Postcode . . . .

Daytime Tel No . . . .

Email . . . .

ISBN 1-85937-995-8   Valid to 31/12/08

Free Print – see overleaf

Can you help us with information about any of the Frith photographs in this book?

We are gradually compiling an historical record for each of the photographs in the Frith archive. It is always fascinating to find out the names of the people shown in the pictures, as well as insights into the shops, buildings and other features depicted.

If you recognize anyone in the photographs in this book, or if you have information not already included in the author's caption, do let us know. We would love to hear from you, and will try to publish it in future books or articles.

Our production team

Frith books are produced by a small dedicated team at offices in the converted Grade II listed 18th-century barn at Teffont near Salisbury, illustrated above. Most have worked with the Frith Collection for many years. All have in common one quality: they have a passion for the Frith Collection. The team is constantly expanding, but currently includes:

Andrew Alsop, Paul Baron, Jason Buck, John Buck, Heather Crisp, David Davies, Natalie Davis, Louis du Mont, Isobel Hall, Chris Hardwick, Lucy Hart, Julian Hight, Peter Horne, James Kinnear, Karen Kinnear, Tina Leary, Stuart Login, Sue Molloy, Miles Murray, Sarah Roberts, Kate Rotondetto, Dean Scource, Eliza Sackett, Terence Sackett, Sandra Sampson, Adrian Sanders, Sandra Sanger, Julia Skinner, Lewis Taylor, Shelley Tolcher, Lorraine Tuck, Miranda Tunnicliffe, Will Tunnicliffe, David Turner and Ricky Williams.